OCEAN LIFE UP CLOSE

Puffer Fish

by Rebecca Pettiford

BLASTOFF! READERS

3

BELLWETHER MEDIA • MINNEAPOLIS, MN

Note to Librarians, Teachers, and Parents:

Blastoff! Readers are carefully developed by literacy experts and combine standards-based content with developmentally appropriate text.

Level 1 provides the most support through repetition of high-frequency words, light text, predictable sentence patterns, and strong visual support.

Level 2 offers early readers a bit more challenge through varied simple sentences, increased text load, and less repetition of high-frequency words.

Level 3 advances early-fluent readers toward fluency through increased text and concept load, less reliance on visuals, longer sentences, and more literary language.

Level 4 builds reading stamina by providing more text per page, increased use of punctuation, greater variation in sentence patterns, and increasingly challenging vocabulary.

Level 5 encourages children to move from "learning to read" to "reading to learn" by providing even more text, varied writing styles, and less familiar topics.

Whichever book is right for your reader, Blastoff! Readers are the perfect books to build confidence and encourage a love of reading that will last a lifetime!

This edition first published in 2017 by Bellwether Media, Inc.

No part of this publication may be reproduced in whole or in part without written permission of the publisher. For information regarding permission, write to Bellwether Media, Inc., Attention: Permissions Department, 5357 Penn Avenue South, Minneapolis, MN 55419.

Library of Congress Cataloging-in-Publication Data

Names: Pettiford, Rebecca, author.
Title: Puffer Fish / by Rebecca Pettiford.
Description: Minneapolis, MN : Bellwether Media, Inc., 2017. | Series: Blastoff! Readers. Ocean Life Up Close | Includes bibliographical references and index. | Audience: Ages 5 to 8. | Audience: Grades K to 3.
Identifiers: LCCN 2016033331 (print) | LCCN 2016042925 (ebook) | ISBN 9781626175723 (hardcover : alk. paper) | ISBN 9781681032931 (ebook)
Subjects: LCSH: Puffers (Fish)–Juvenile literature.
Classification: LCC QL638.T32 P48 2017 (print) | LCC QL638.T32 (ebook) | DDC 597/.64–dc23
LC record available at https://lccn.loc.gov/2016033331

Editor: Christina Leighton   Designer: Brittany McIntosh

Printed in the United States of America, North Mankato, MN.

Table of Contents

Puffer fish swim along warm coasts around the world. There are about 120 types of puffer fish.

Many live in **coral reefs**.
Others live in bays or
mangrove swamps.

Puffer fish are also called puffers or blowfish. They can puff up to two or three times their size.

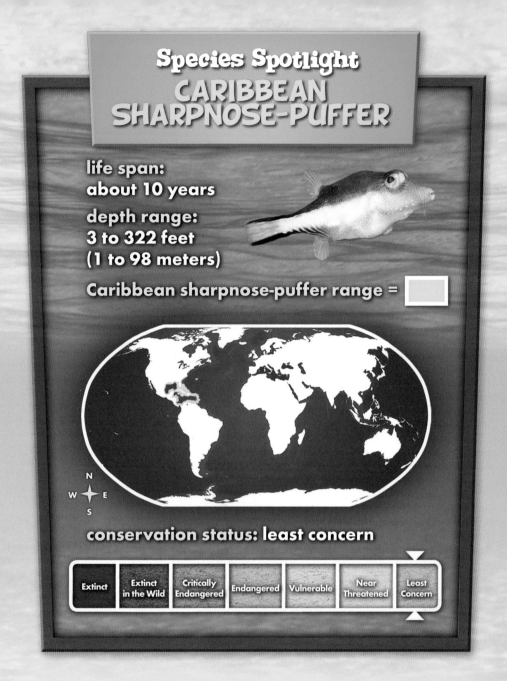

CARIBBEAN SHARPNOSE-PUFFER

life span:
about 10 years

depth range:
3 to 322 feet
(1 to 98 meters)

Caribbean sharpnose-puffer range =

N
W · E
S

conservation status: least concern

Extinct	Extinct in the Wild	Critically Endangered	Endangered	Vulnerable	Near Threatened	Least Concern

They do this by sucking up water or air. Their **elastic** stomachs help them stretch out.

Puffer fish vary in size.
They are between 1 inch
(2.5 centimeters) and
4 feet (1.2 meters) long.

Puffer Fish Sizes

Smallest
dwarf puffer

actual size

1 inch
(2.5 centimeters)
long

Largest
stellate puffer

average
human

4 feet
(1.2 meters)
long

stellate puffer

dwarf puffer

They can weigh up to 30 pounds (13.6 kilograms).

Sharp and Deadly

Puffer fish have tube-shaped bodies. They have large lips and big eyes that stick out.

Valentini's sharpnose puffer

Identify a Puffer Fish

tube-shaped body

big eyes

large lips

Some puffer fish have bright colors and markings. Others have softer colors to blend in with their surroundings.

Puffer fish have a fin on each side
of their bodies. They have smaller
fins near their tails.

These fish are slow swimmers. But they can get away from **predators** in short bursts.

map puffer

Sea Enemies

tiger sharks

bluefin tunas

wahoos

guineafowl puffer

Some puffer fish have smooth bodies. Others have sharp **spines**. These scare predators when the puffer fish puff up.

Most puffer fish are very poisonous. But their poison does not harm hungry tiger sharks.

A Crushing Beak

Most puffer fish are **carnivores**. They often eat **corals** and snails. Some may eat **algae**. Their lips help them search for food.

Puffer fish have four teeth that come together to form a beak. They can crush shells!

Catch of the Day

green algae

lobe corals

flamingo tongue snails

stars and stripes puffer

Baby Puffer Fish

Some male puffer fish make nests on the ocean floor to attract mates. Others guide the females to the ocean surface.

The females release three to seven eggs. The eggs stick to the sand or float in the water.

nest

white-spotted puffer fish

Baby puffer fish **hatch** within six days. The babies are called **larvae**.

They are born with a hard shell
that protects them. When the shell
breaks, they swim to safety!

Glossary

algae—plants and plantlike living things; most kinds of algae grow in water.

carnivores—animals that only eat meat

coral reefs—structures made of coral that usually grow in shallow seawater

corals—the living ocean animals that build coral reefs

elastic—able to stretch and then return to the original size and shape

hatch—to break out of an egg

larvae—early, tiny forms of an animal that must go through a big change to become adults

mangrove swamps—coastal saltwater wetlands filled with tropical trees called mangroves

predators—animals that hunt other animals for food

spines—sharp body parts that some puffer fish have around their body

To Learn More

AT THE LIBRARY

Leigh, Autumn. *Deadly Pufferfish*. New York, N.Y.: Gareth Stevens Publishing, 2011.

Markovics, Joyce. *Puffer Fish*. New York, N.Y.: Bearport Publishing, 2016.

Rudenko, Dennis. *Look Out for the Pufferfish!* New York, N.Y.: PowerKids Press, 2016.

ON THE WEB

Learning more about puffer fish is as easy as 1, 2, 3.

1. Go to www.factsurfer.com.

2. Enter "puffer fish" into the search box.

3. Click the "Surf" button and you will see a list of related web sites.

With factsurfer.com, finding more information is just a click away.

Index

The images in this book are reproduced through the courtesy of: Moize nicolas, front cover, p. 6; bearacreative, p. 3; Rich Carey, pp. 4, 5, 11 (top right); Stubblefield Photography, p. 7; Bildagentur Zoonar GmbH, p. 9 (top); blickwinkel/ Alamy, p. 9 (bottom); WaterFrame/ Alamy, p. 10; Richard Whitcombe, p. 11 (top left); JonMilnes, p. 11 (top center); serg_dibrova, p. 11 (bottom); Michael Herman, p. 12; Michael Stubblefield/ Alamy, p. 13; Matt9122, p. 14 (top left); holbox (top center); Neophuket, p. 14 (top right); David Fleetham/ Alamy, p. 14 (bottom); ligio, p. 15; Aleksandar Mijatovic, p. 17 (top left); David Witherall and Jema Warta/ Wikipedia, p. 17 (top center); Seaphotoart, p. 17 (top right); Georgette Douwma/ Science Source, p. 17 (bottom); Norbert Probst/ imageBROKER/ SuperStock, p. 18; Yoji Okata/ Minden Pictures, p. 19 (top, bottom); Universal Images Group/ SuperStock, p. 20; Laura Dinraths, p. 21.